S0-AWF-640

Grade 6

KUMON WRITING WORKBOOKS

Writing

Table of Contents

KUMON

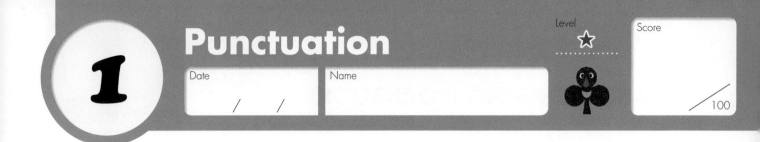

Punctuation

1 Trace the colon in each sentence. Then read the sentence aloud.

5 points each

(1) We bought quite a few things for Fred's party : balloons, drinks, and cutlery.

(2) Leaders from the following countries arrived : Canada, Honduras, and Venezuela.

(3) The plan had to be kept a secret : The party was supposed to be a surprise.

(4) The price of grapes varies : The cost depends on whether the fruit is in season.

Don't forget!

A **colon (:)** is most often used to introduce a list of items.
   For example: The salad had many ingredients: tomatoes, peppers, oil, and cheese.

A colon is also used to join two clauses. The second clause gives an explanation or more information about the first clause. If the second clause is an independent clause, the first letter is capitalized.
   For example: The judge was firm about his ruling: There would be no appeal.

---

2 Combine each sentence pair with a colon.

10 points each

(1) Lizzie bought spices for the curry. She got cumin, curry powder, and cardamom.

Lizzie bought spices for the curry <u>: cumin, curry powder, and cardamom</u> .

(2) We learned a lot from Mr. Hall. He taught us loyalty, honesty, and teamwork.

_____

(3) You can avoid the flu by taking simple precautions. Avoid the flu by washing your hands, avoiding sick people, and not touching your face.

_____

_____

3 Read the passage. Combine one pair of sentences from each paragraph with a colon.

15 points each

Daniel's father decided that Daniel's new pup would sleep outside. Daniel lobbied his father for a doghouse, and in the end his father relented. In fact, they became excited about building the doghouse together. Daniel was happy. He knew that his dog would have a roof over its head.

They needed six items to start. They needed nails, wood, glue, roofing, sealant, and paint. Daniel's father agreed to buy the materials. It was a beautiful day, but Daniel couldn't help thinking about all the cool nights ahead in the fall. He added "carpet" and "bed" to the list. That would make the dog feel better when the nights were cool.

They bought all of the materials and headed home to get started. They picked an area in the backyard that made the most sense for a doghouse. They set up the saw and all of the tools they needed, then laid out their plan. They worked for the rest of the afternoon, until Daniel hammered the last nail. The moment had arrived. The dog entered its new home and laid down. Daniel high-fived his dad.

(1) Daniel was happy:

(2)

(3)

4 Write your own sentence using all of the words from the box and a colon.

5 points for completion

recipe   ingredients   tomatoes   onions

Great start!

2 Punctuation

Level ☆

Score /100

Date / /

Name

---

1 Trace the semicolon in each sentence. Then read the sentence aloud.

5 points each

(1) I wanted him to apologize to our friend_;_ he agreed.

(2) He learned how to fish_;_ he can catch his dinner.

(3) She was absolutely bored_;_ nevertheless, she continued watching the movie.

(4) The girl had not learned to read yet_;_ however, she flipped through the book.

> **Don't forget!**
>
> A **semicolon (;)** is used to join two independent clauses. A semicolon shows that there is a close relationship between the two clauses.
>   For example: We will have company tonight; we are cleaning to prepare for them.
>
> A semicolon is also used when the second independent clause begins with a transition word, such as *however*, *therefore*, or *furthermore*.
>   For example: We tried to finish in time; *however*, the guests arrived early.

2 Combine each sentence pair with a semicolon and the conjunction in the brackets.

10 points each

(1) Sojourner Truth could neither read nor write. She could give speeches.
[however]

_____

_____

(2) The golfer practiced much more. He won the championship.
[hence]

_____

_____

(3) He was afraid of the dark. He shrieked when the power went out.
[therefore]

_____

_____

3 Read the passage. Combine one pair of sentences from each paragraph with a semicolon.

15 points per question

Dustin was always told that he was too small. He liked to play basketball, but classmates said he couldn't even be a point guard at his height. He wanted to be a pitcher on the baseball team, but players said that pitchers are tall. He didn't have the stature that most athletes have. Hence, he was told that he couldn't succeed in sports.

Yet, he was determined, so he practiced every day, with or without friends. He trained so intensely that his coaches finally started giving him playing time. He didn't get to be a pitcher, but he did become the starting shortstop on his baseball team. He also played point guard on the school basketball team. He was happy. Everyone had told him it was impossible. Nevertheless, he persevered.

Dustin didn't want his dreams to end there, though. He had a goal of making it big as a professional athlete, despite being small for his age even as he grew older. When scouts arrived at a game, they ignored him. Indeed, they thought he was too small for college baseball. But then they saw him play. Dustin's hard work paid off, and he outshined every other player on the field. Dustin was given many offers after that. Today, Dustin is an all-star second baseman in professional baseball.

(1) _____

_____

(2) _____

_____

(3) _____

_____

4 Write your own sentence using all of the words from the box and a semicolon.

5 points for completion

| small | determination | however | big | dreams |

_____

_____

_____

You're doing well!

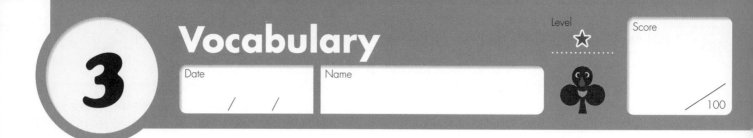

Vocabulary

Date   /   /

Name

Level ☆

Score   /100

1 Match each definition with a word from the passage.

5 points each

Two monks smuggle silkworm eggs out of the village. One smuggler hides the silkworm eggs in his cane.

(1) _____   (verb) to bring into or take out of a place secretly, often illegally

(2) _____   (noun) a person who brings things into or out of a place secretly, often illegally

Don't forget!

The **dictionary form of a noun** is always singular.
    For example: The <u>smugglers</u> hide.
        Smuggler is the dictionary form.
The **dictionary form of a verb** is always the infinitive, or the "to" form, without the word *to*.
    For example: She <u>walks</u> away.
        To walk is the infinitive form. *Walk* is the dictionary form.

2 Convert each verb to its dictionary form.

5 points each

(1) talked: _____

(2) playing: _____

(3) liked: _____

(4) shouts: _____

3 Match each definition with a word from the passage. Convert the word to its dictionary form if necessary.

10 points each

My shirt has embroidery on it. Janice embroidered her jacket with blue and gold thread.

(1) _____   (verb) to decorate fabric with patterns sewn in colored thread

(2) _____   (noun) patterns sewn in colored thread onto fabric

4 Match each definition with a word from the sentence. Convert the word to its dictionary form if necessary.

5 points each

(1) Merchants sold their goods in bazaars in Damascus and Baghdad.

_____ (noun) a person who buys and sells goods

(2) Camels were used to carry merchandise across the desert.

_____ (noun) goods for sale

(3) People continue to search for extraterrestrial life.

_____ (adjective) of or relating to things outside the planet Earth

(4) Despite the secrecy surrounding silk production, people in other countries found out how to make it.

_____ (noun) the state of being kept hidden or secret

(5) The cook was secretive about how his stew was made.

_____ (adjective) not open to telling people things

(6) Hikers can travel through many different terrains in California.

_____ (noun) land and its natural features

5 Write each noun as an adjective.

5 points each

(1) fear: _____fearful_____

(2) anger: _____

(3) secrecy: _____

(4) cheer: _____

Awesome work!

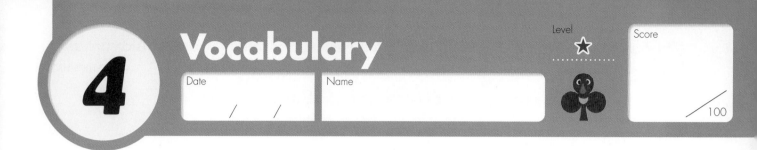
1 Match each definition with a word from the sentences in the box. Convert the word to its dictionary form if necessary.

5 points each

> Batteries cannot hold a charge forever.
>
> Power plants create electricity in machines called generators.
>
> Math problems can be solved by using a calculator.
>
> Lightning discharges the electricity that builds up in clouds.
>
> Most power plants use coal, oil, or natural gas to generate electricity.
>
> Benjamin Franklin took a calculated risk when he flew his kite in a thunderstorm.

(1) ___generate___ (verb) to create or produce

(2) _____ (noun) a machine that converts mechanical energy into electrical energy

(3) _____ (noun) the amount of electricity stored by something

(4) _____ (verb) to release; to allow to leave

(5) _____ (adjective) planned carefully in advance

(6) _____ (noun) a device used to perform mathematical calculations

2 Complete the word group.

10 points each

(1) calculate (verb) to solve a problem, often mathematically

calculated (adjective) planned carefully in advance

_____ (noun) a device used to solve mathematical calculations

(2) charge (noun) the amount of electricity stored by something

charged (adjective) showing strong emotion; excited

_____ (verb) to load with electricity

3 Match each definition with a word from the sentences in the box. Convert the word to its dictionary form if necessary.

5 points each

> Peter has wonderfully expressive eyes.
>
> Javier wrote a concise summary of the book.
>
> Winning the tournament was one of his greatest accomplishments.
>
> While some artworks represent real life, others are more abstract.
>
> Michelangelo took four years to paint the ceiling of the Sistine Chapel, which was a task that he largely accomplished alone.
>
> The expression on her face was totally different from the one she wore only moments before.

(1) _____ (adjective) not based on reality

(2) _____ (adjective) giving a lot of information clearly and in a few words

(3) _____ (adjective) showing emotion

(4) _____ (noun) an act of feeling; something which shows feeling

(5) _____ (noun) an achievement

(6) _____ (verb) to achieve or complete something

4 Complete the word group.

10 points each

(1) celebrated   (adjective) honored or praised

_____ (noun) someone famous

(2) magnetic   (adjective) having the power to attract metal objects

_____ (noun) a piece of metal that attracts other metal objects

Super effort!

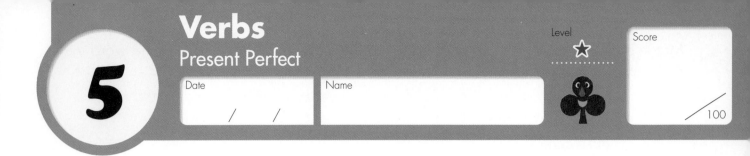

Verbs
Present Perfect

5

Date / /

Name

Level

Score

/100

1 Complete the chart.

5 points each

Present Tense	Present Perfect Tense
walk / walks	have / has walked
(1) __move / moves__	have / has moved
use / uses	(2) _____
improve / improves	(3) _____
(4) _____	have / has built
remind / reminds	(5) _____
make / makes	(6) _____

> **Don't forget!**
>
> The **present perfect tense** of a verb is used to describe an action that occurred in the past and is related to the present time or to indicate that an action begun in the past is ongoing in the present. It is formed with the helping verb *have* or *has* and the past participle of the verb.
> For example: I <u>study</u>. / I <u>have studied</u> a lot for this test.
>   present   present perfect

2 Complete each sentence with the present or present perfect tense of the verb in the brackets.

5 points each

(1) I _____ the window when it is raining. [close]

She _____ the window already.

(2) My little sister _____ her homework every day. [finish]

She _____ her homework already.

(3) James _____ through that magazine each month. [browse]

He _____ through all the books by now.

(4) The surgeon _____ on her patient. [operate]

The surgeon _____ on many patients successfully.

3 Rewrite each sentence in the present perfect tense.

5 points each

(1) Mom starts her job.

_____

(2) Jonah slices bread for sandwiches.

_____

(3) The realtor sells many houses.

_____

(4) I finish my homework for tomorrow.

_____

(5) I turn off the lights.

_____

4 Complete each sentence with a word or words from the brackets.

5 points each

(1) The tailor _____ or cut the fabric yet.

[has not measured / will not be measuring]

(2) I _____ the way this dish turned out this time.

[dislike / have disliked]

(3) Juan _____ and ruined the meat.

[has scorched / scorches]

(4) Carl _____ and fallen to the ground.

[has stumbled / stumbled]

(5) The tulips bulbs we planted a few days ago _____ already.

[have sprouted / sprout]

Nice job!

Verbs
Past Perfect

6

Level ☆

Score

/100

Date   /   /

Name

1 Complete the chart.

5 points each

Past Tense	Past Perfect Tense
discussed	had discussed
(1)_____	had dislodged
fashioned	(2)_____
agreed	(3)_____
(4)_____	had eaten
read	(5)_____
sprained	(6)_____

Don't forget!

The **past perfect tense** is used to express an action that was completed before another event or before a specified time. The past perfect tense is formed with the helping verb *had* and the past participle of the verb.

For example: He <u>had not visited</u> New York City before he <u>was</u> a teenager.
                 past perfect   past

2 Complete each sentence with the past or past perfect tense of the verb in the brackets.

5 points each

(1) I _____ the window before I turned on the air conditioner.　　[close]

(2) The sled dogs had run twenty-five miles before they _____ the finish line.　　[cross]

(3) We _____ with ice cream after our team had won the championship.　　[celebrate]

(4) Julie had never seen a shooting star before she _____ one tonight.　　[see]

3 Rewrite each sentence in the past perfect tense.   5 points each

(1) The mirror reflected the light.

_____

(2) The game stopped because of rain.

_____

(3) The tree concealed the big house.

_____

(4) Maria demonstrated the problem.

_____

(5) Mom thought I could make my lunch.

_____

4 Complete each sentence with a word or words from the brackets.   5 points each

(1) The audience _____ the concert hall as the opening band played.

[filled / had filled]

(2) Jennifer _____ any spelling errors as she wrote her essay.

[didn't make / had not made]

(3) Mel _____ the files accidentally before we could find the data.

[deleted / had deleted]

(4) Joe _____ before Brian admitted guilt.

[didn't confess / had not confessed]

(5) The boat _____ the goods before departing for another port.

[delivered / had delivered]

Keep it up!

© Kumon Publishing Co., Ltd.   13

Verbs
Future Perfect

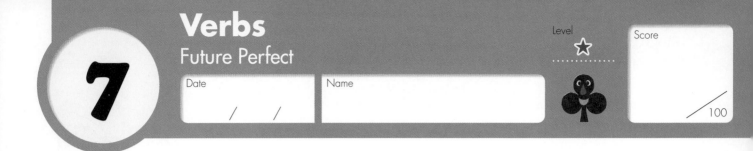

Level

Score

Date   /   /

Name

/ 100

1 Complete the chart.

5 points each

Future Tense	Future Perfect Tense
will watch	will have watched
(1)_____	will have walked
will support	(2)_____
will contain	(3)_____
(4)_____	will have sung
will finish	(5)_____
will win	(6)_____

Don't forget!

The **future perfect tense** is used to express an action that is currently happening and will be completed before a specific time. The future perfect tense is formed by the helping verbs *will have* and the past participle of the verb.

For example: By the end of the week, I <u>will have sold</u> all my tickets.
future perfect

2 Complete each sentence with the future or future perfect tense of the verb in the brackets.

5 points each

(1) By morning, Phil _____ eight hours.   [sleep]

(2) James _____ his room later this morning.   [clean]

(3) Eno _____ many seashells after walking along the beach.   [collect]

(4) The child _____ all the books by the time he leaves.   [read]

3 Rewrite each sentence in the future perfect tense.

5 points each

(1) Mom works all week.

By Friday, _____.

(2) Steven collected ten baseball cards.

This week alone, Steven _____

_____.

(3) I will practice for an hour.

By four o'clock, _____.

(4) The crew demolished the building.

By the end of today, the crew _____

_____.

(5) He uses all of the soap.

To clean every dish, he _____.

4 Complete each sentence with a word or words from the brackets.

5 points each

(1) Jacob is biking all over the city. By the time he gets home, he _____ for
three hours.   [biked / will have biked]

(2) That butterfly has fluttered around me for a while. By sunset, it _____ around
me for many hours.   [fluttered / will have fluttered]

(3) Nate's brother _____ him yesterday. Nate's brother has always been a
good teacher.   [tutored / has tutored / will have tutored]

(4) The king has reigned for a long time. By next year, he _____ for
a half-century.   [reigned / has reigned / will have reigned]

(5) You can call me at home at 8:00 p.m. I _____ there by then.
                                  [arrived / have arrived / will have arrived]

Exceptional work!

Review
Verbs

Level ☆

Score

/ 100

Date   /   /

Name

8

1 Complete each sentence with the verb in the indicated tense.   10 points each

(1) **walk**

Henry _____ around this lake already.   (present perfect)

Henry _____ around the lake before it froze.   (past perfect)

Henry _____ around the lake three times by tonight.   (future perfect)

(2) **promote**

The movie star _____ her film.   (present perfect)

The movie star _____ her film before the premiere.   (past perfect)

The movie star _____ her film before it is in theaters.   (future perfect)

(3) **demonstrate**

You _____ the law of gravity well.   (present perfect)

You _____ the law of gravity before I did.   (past perfect)

You _____ the law of gravity by the end of class.   (future perfect)

2 Rewrite each sentence in the indicated tense.   5 points each

(1) We hiked through the sun-speckled forest.

_____

(present perfect)

(2) The boy camped all summer.

_____

(future perfect)

(3) Napoleon's army forced a retreat.

_____

(past perfect)

(4) Lightning strikes a tree in the yard.

_____

(present perfect)

3 Complete each sentence with a word or words from the brackets. 5 points each

(1) Moe wasn't sure where his book was. He _____ around his room for it but did not see it.

[has glanced / had glanced]

(2) The track meet has many events. By the end of the meet, Bo _____ in four separate events.

[will have raced / raced]

(3) The emergency workers _____ the spilled oil before it contaminated the drinking water.

[had contained / have contained]

(4) Wind turbines generate a small part of the world's energy. In 2009,

they _____ only 2 percent of the world's energy.

[will have generated / had generated]

4 Complete each sentence with the verb in the appropriate tense. 10 points each

(1) **clean**
Mom came upstairs expecting our room to be dirty, but we _____ it already.

(2) **delete**
Mrs. Zimmermann asked for the essay, but I _____ some files accidentally and couldn't find it.

(3) **sew**
Grandma has fixed most of my little sister's dolls. By tomorrow, she _____ more than twenty dolls!

Keep it going!

Review
Verbs

9

Level ☆

Score

/100

Date / /

Name

1 Read the passage. Then write the letter representing each sentence next to its verb tense.

10 points each

Fashion began with people's desire to demonstrate their wealth or power. [A] Governments even created laws to control what people were allowed to wear. In sixteenth-century England, Henry VIII introduced a law that prohibited anyone of low rank from wearing luxury fabrics like silk. [B] He had believed it was important that a person's dress be associated with his or her position in life.

Like many things, fashion evolves, and sometimes certain items of clothing can take on entirely new functions at different times and places. For example, the kimono is a traditional dress worn in Japan. After being transported to the West in the seventeenth century, [C] this garment has developed into what we know today as a dressing gown or bathrobe.

Some modern fashions actually date back to antiquity. Before the twentieth century, swimsuits generally concealed most of the body. When the bikini was introduced in 1947, it was considered so outrageous that models refused to wear it. The bikini was not a new idea, however, but a reinvention of a garment that first appeared nearly two thousand years earlier. [D] In some societies, bikinis will have gone in and out of fashion for centuries.

(1) past: _____

(2) present perfect: _____

(3) future perfect: _____

(4) past perfect: _____

2 Complete each sentence with the verb in the indicated tense.

5 points each

(1) **become** (present perfect & negative)
Motorcycles have become safer over the years, but they _have not become_ safer than cars.

(2) **collect** (past perfect & negative)
Lori had collected many baseball cards in her youth, but she _____ as many as her brother.

3 Rewrite each sentence in the indicated tense.

5 points each

(1) Eli finishes all his chores. (past perfect & negative)

Eli had not finished all his chores.

(2) Ignacio had an eventful winter. (past perfect & negative)

_____

(3) The company pays its taxes each year. (present perfect & negative)

_____

(4) The child listens to the story. (past perfect & negative)

_____

4 Complete the final sentence of each passage with the verb in the appropriate tense. You can use the negative form as well.

10 points each

(1) **break**

Julian is an unlucky guy—at least when it comes to breaking bones. He has broken his leg, his wrist, and his right arm. He even fractured his pinkie finger once. His sister Julie is the opposite. She _____ a bone.

(2) **decide**

Bill had just sat down to eat cereal when his mother began cleaning out the refrigerator. She found a moldy slice of pizza and something unidentifiable.

Bill asked, "Is the milk spoiled?"

"Yes, it definitely is," she said.

Bill looked down at his bowl and then pushed it away. He _____ he was no longer hungry.

(3) **own**

The American car manufacturer Henry Ford improved the assembly line model and added the first factory conveyor belt. The first Model T Ford was produced on August 12, 1908, and the first four-door version was introduced in 1926. The four-door car has been very popular. By 2026, Americans _____ four-door cars for one hundred years.

Fantastic job!

10

Level ★

Score / 100

Date / /

Name

1 Complete each sentence with an independent clause from the box.

5 points each

I went swimming	we were never late
we could not get a clear signal	The UFO landed

(1) _____ and then dried off.

(2) Since we lived so close to school, _____.

(3) _____ before the newscast could alert people.

(4) Until we replaced the antenna, _____.

Hint: An **independent clause** can stand alone as a sentence and is a complete thought. An independent clause includes a subject and a predicate.

For example: Before we went outside, <u>our teacher gave us a soccer ball.</u>

independent clause

2 Circle the independent clause in each sentence.

6 points each

(1) Because I missed the bus, I was late for school.

(2) When I finally got to school, the class was already working quietly.

(3) Everyone stared at me but didn't say a thing.

(4) The teacher did not give me detention because this was the first time I was late.

(5) If I arrive late again tomorrow, I will surely get detention.

3 Write the independent clause of each sentence as a simple sentence.   5 points each

(1) Sam will go to the party as long as you go, too.

_____

(2) The substitute teacher said that we could not leave until the assignment was finished.

_____

(3) If only I had remembered, I would have returned the movie.

_____

(4) After the hockey game ends, we will go out for hamburgers.

_____

4 If the underlined clause in each sentence is independent, write a check mark on the line.

5 points each

(1) Since I met you, <u>I have been to many new places</u>.   _____

(2) <u>Even though her team won</u>, Jenny felt she hadn't played her best.   _____

(3) <u>I called my grandmother</u> because she was not feeling well.   _____

(4) In case you need it, <u>here is Gigi's phone number</u>.   _____

(5) <u>Although we were tired</u>, we went to Becca's concert.   _____

(6) <u>While Ted was not home</u>, a squirrel got into the house.   _____

You are excellent!

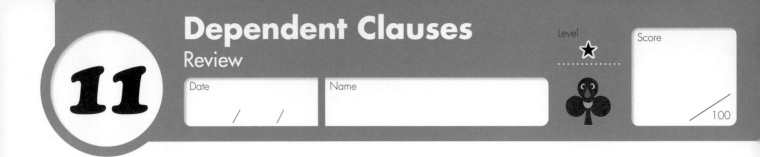

Dependent Clauses
Review

Date   /   /

Name

1   Write the noun clause of each sentence.   5 points each

(1) The screenwriter was hoping that the movie would become a hit.

that the movie would become a hit

(2) Jennifer asked her mother why the sunset was so colorful.

_____

(3) A test driver will determine how the motorcycle handles bad conditions.

_____

(4) The gymnast showed us how to do a back handspring.

_____

(5) That he was found guilty made the movie's ending tragic.

_____

2   Complete each sentence with an adverb clause from the box.   5 points each

until she found an illustration   before cars could become widespread
as she describes her home   although it mentions real people
as though life were an adventure

(1) The book is fiction _____.

(2) The girl flipped through the pages _____.

(3) The pirate Long John Silver acted _____.

(4) Advances in manufacturing were necessary _____

_____.

(5) _____, the writer uses images from her memories.

3 Write the adjective clause of each sentence.

5 points each

(1) This is the school where I study art.

where I study art

(2) The lecture that the professor gave put everyone to sleep.

_____

(3) The students who received training found jobs.

_____

Hint: A **noun clause** is a dependent clause that acts as a noun. An **adverb clause** is a dependent clause that acts as an adverb. An **adjective clause** is a dependent clause that acts as an adjective.

(4) In courtroom mysteries, someone who appears guilty is often proven innocent.

_____

(5) The Daytona 200 is a major motorcycle race that is held on the same track as the Daytona 500 auto race.

_____

_____

4 Underline the independent clause of each sentence. Circle the dependent clause. Then write the type of dependent clause: adjective, adverb, or noun clause.

5 points each

(1) The building now has ramps that students in wheelchairs use.

_____

(2) The article reports that the man on trial was not guilty.

_____

(3) Before writing was developed, people communicated with smoke signals, drums, and whistles.

_____

(4) The pollution that results from car exhaust causes major harm to our environment.

_____

(5) My brother wondered where all our friends had gone.

_____

You really know your stuff!

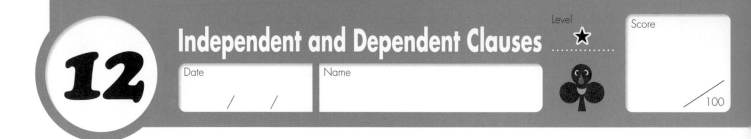

Independent and Dependent Clauses

Level ★

Date / /

Name

Score /100

1 Complete the paragraph with the dependent and independent clauses from the box.

10 points each

> who always try to keep us from fighting
> She explained that my list had convinced her
> I took my time reading and writing about my sister's choice
> Before I could speak
> where to go for our family vacation

This year, my parents let the kids choose (1)_____

_____.

(2)_____, my sister shouted that

she wanted to go to the beach. I quickly said that I was hoping we

could go to a theme park. My parents, (3)_____

_____,

suggested that we each write down a list of pros and cons for our

own choice. After we made our lists, our parents asked us to swap

lists and add to each other's pros and cons list.

(4)_____

_____,

but she seemed to finish very quickly. When it was time to show our

parents what we had written, I was surprised to see that my sister

hadn't added anything to my theme park list. (5)_____

_____,

and now she wanted to go to a theme park, too!

2 Complete the paragraph with compound sentences. Write each compound sentence with an independent clause from the left column, a comma and conjunction, and an independent clause from the right column.

10 points each

Independent Clauses	Conjunctions	Independent Clauses
My friends think Sunny is more like a dog than a cat.	but	Sunny can do many tricks.
For example, she meows at strangers.		She loves to catch a ball.
	and	My mom won't let me feed her.
Most cats will not perform tricks.		I agree.
She begs under the dinner table.	so	I keep her in my room when guests come by.
Sunny also plays fetch.		

My cat, Sunny, is a very unusual cat. She will do tricks, act strangely, and eat things that no normal cat would eat. (1) _Most cats will not perform tricks, but Sunny can do many tricks._ For instance, Sunny comes when I call her name.
(2) _____

_____ Sometimes Sunny can

be very loud. (3) _____

_____

_____ Unlike most

picky cats, Sunny loves to eat just about anything. (4) _____

_____

_____

Every now and then, I sneak her a small meatball. (5) _____

_____

_____

Hint: A **compound sentence** contains two independent clauses joined together by a comma and a conjunction.

You make this look easy!

25

Independent and Dependent Clauses

Level ☆ ....

Score

Date   /   /

Name

/100

1 Read the paragraph. Write the independent clause of each underlined sentence as a complete sentence.

6 points each

(1)<u>Singing is my passion, so I have studied it since I was very young.</u> I take singing lessons two times a week at a school for the performing arts. I practice my music nightly. (2)<u>Because I sing so often, I take care of my voice.</u> (3)<u>Whenever it is possible, I try not to talk or yell loudly.</u> My best friend is also a singer. (4)<u>Although I love singing, I avoid competing with her for solos.</u> Fortunately, we have different goals. (5)<u>She is auditioning for the school's musical, while I want to sing the lead in the glee club.</u> I am so glad to have a friend who shares my passion for singing.

(1) Singing is my passion.

(2) _____

(3) _____

(4) _____

(5) _____

2 Write the type of dependent clause in each sentence: adjective, adverb, or noun clause.

5 points each

(1) Jeremy couldn't participate <u>because of his knee injury</u>.   _____

(2) The dancer <u>whom we saw perform last night</u> just walked by!   _____

(3) I can't understand <u>why you didn't want to go to the party</u>.   _____

(4) He can jump farther <u>than I can</u>.   _____

3 Underline the dependent clause in each sentence. Then write the type of dependent clause.

5 points each

(1) This is the closet where they keep all the costumes. _____

(2) James asked me why I make scrapbooks. _____

(3) Before I joined the team, I watched too much television. _____

(4) The chemist showed us how rust forms. _____

4 Complete each sentence in your own words with the indicated type of dependent clause.

5 points each

(1) As _____, we whistled a tune.

[adverb clause]

(2) The shirt _that_ _____ was wrinkled.

[adjective clause]

(3) She sat up straight _before_ _____.

[adverb clause]

(4) We talked with the students _who_ _____.

[adjective clause]

(5) A quiz is a test of _what_ _____.

[noun clause]

(6) I hope _that_ _____.

[noun clause]

Great work!

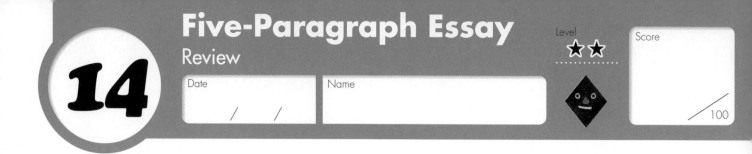

Five-Paragraph Essay
Review

Level ★★

Score

Date / /

Name

/100

1 Read the five-paragraph essay. Label each paragraph, section, or underlined sentence with a description from the box on page 29. You can use each description more than once.

100 points for completion

(2)____

"Make a movie in your mind." Teachers tell students this to help them visualize a story's action. Indeed, many books are made into movies, but many people don't even know the adapted books exist! (7)____ <u>I think you should read a book before watching its movie version for three reasons:</u> When you read the book first, you get the author's original vision of the story. Also, reading allows you to create your own visual representation of the story and characters in your mind. Lastly, the book usually delves deeper into the story than the movie can.

(3)____

(8)____ <u>As previously mentioned, the book offers the author's original idea of the story.</u> When a book is made into a movie, many elements are often changed. Characters may be added or changed substantially. Often, scenes are cut in order to save time. Sometimes, the setting or time period is changed in order to make the movie more relevant to a certain audience. By only seeing the movie version, you could miss out on a lot of what the author has tried to say.

(1)____ (4)____

(9)____ <u>Besides all the changes that occur when a book is adapted into a movie,</u> as a movie viewer, you miss the opportunity to imagine the story for yourself. One of the greatest pleasures of reading is the activity of imagining the story. When you watch a movie, the work is being done for you. (10)____ <u>The director, cinematographer, casting director, and many other people involved in creating a film control the visual representation instead.</u> If you then decide to read the book, you will have the movie's images in mind.

(5)____

Also, movies cannot include the same amount of detail as books. (11)____ <u>Most movies are under two hours long, so detailed parts of a book must be cut.</u> Also, the thoughts and feelings of many characters are often included in a book but not explained in a film. (12)____ <u>The high cost of producing a movie prevents the makers from including all the background information on characters or places.</u> When you watch the movie version of a book instead of reading it, you are not getting the same detailed story.

(6)____

(13)____ <u>To summarize, you should read the book before going to see the movie.</u> Movies change the author's original story, you don't get to imagine the visual scenes for yourself, and movies can't include all the details that a book can. (14)____ <u>To conclude, by reading a book before seeing the movie, you enjoy a better experience with the story.</u>

(A)   Introductory paragraph

(B)   Body

(C)   Supporting paragraph

(D)   Conclusion

(E)   Topic sentence

(F)   Supporting detail

(G)   Transition sentence or phrase

(H)   Concluding sentence

(I)   Restatement of the topic sentence

Hint: A **topic sentence** is a sentence that describes what an essay or paragraph is mostly about. The introductory paragraph of a five-paragraph essay usually begins with a topic sentence that states the essay's main idea and the supporting paragraphs' main ideas. Each supporting paragraph will also include a topic sentence elaborating its main ideas.

Hint: A **five-paragraph essay** is a passage that is organized into five paragraphs. The **introductory paragraph** is the first paragraph. It states the main idea of the passage in its topic sentence. The **body** is made up of the **supporting paragraphs**, or the second, third, and fourth paragraphs. They give details on the topic and evidence to support the main idea. The **conclusion** is the fifth paragraph. It summarizes the essay and reinforces the ideas given in the introductory paragraph and body.

You are ready to write.

Five-Paragraph Essay
Review

15

Level ⭐⭐

Score
/100

Date / /

Name

1 Complete the five-paragraph essay with the sentences and phrases from the box on page 31.

10 points each

Wind tunnels simulate the movement of air around an aircraft in flight and are a very useful tool for testing new aircraft. While the model aircraft is inside a wind tunnel, an engineer can control the environment and simulate real-life conditions. He or she then can gather data about how the aircraft performed under those conditions. (1)_____

_____

With all these benefits, wind tunnels play an important part in the development of new aircraft.

In order to simulate the conditions a plane may endure, (2)_____

_____

Wind tunnels come in a variety of sizes. (3)_____

_____ The fans can move the air at under 200 miles per hour to faster than the speed of sound. Usually a small-scale version of the plane—or even spacecraft—is placed in the tunnel and fixed in place so it cannot move. The force of air around the aircraft replicates (4)_____

_____

_____ Sometimes engineers put the full-size vehicle or a piece of the vehicle in the wind tunnel, depending on what they are testing.

(5)_____

_____

_____ These instruments measure the forces produced by the air on the plane. Also, by injecting smoke or dye into the tunnel and photographing the flow of the air, engineers can also study how the air moves around the aircraft. (6)_____

_____

By carefully recording all the data from the model, (7)_____

_____

With the additional information, the engineer can even improve the performance and durability of the aircraft. (8)_____

_____

_____

(9)_____

By using a wind tunnel, the conditions an aircraft might experience in flight can be simulated, and an engineer can gather a lot of helpful information. This research could lead to discoveries and, eventually, to new and improved designs. By performing these tests in wind tunnels,

(10)_____

_____

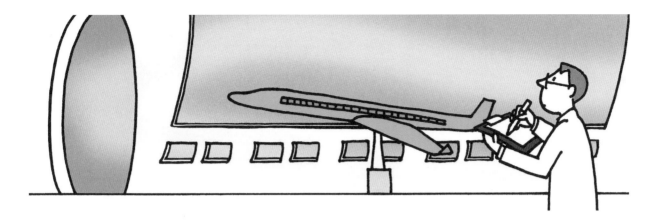

They gather as much data as possible from these experiments for later examination.

what would happen if the aircraft were flying.

A wind tunnel is a powerful instrument for researchers.

Then, the engineer can use that information to improve the aircraft's design.

engineers have the ability to improve air travel and make great discoveries.

Wind tunnels also move air at different speeds.

When engineers build the model version of the aircraft, they include special instruments to take measurements during the wind tunnel test.

an engineer can predict how a full-size aircraft will perform.

For example, an engineer might improve the flow of air around a vehicle to increase its lift and decrease resistance that slows it down.

engineers choose specific wind tunnels and adjust the powerful fans.

You're flying now!

Five-Paragraph Essay
Review

Date   /   /   Name

1 Complete each essay topics by brainstorming main ideas in your own words.   14 points each

(1)
I would like to live _____ one day.
in New York City
on a farm
on a boat

_____
_____

(2)
If I could enact a law, I would…
make college mandatory
make vacations mandatory
make community service mandatory

_____
_____

(3)
The most important environmental problem is…
oil spills
pollution
the dwindling rain forest

_____
_____

(4)
One way my town could improve is by…
building a better library
adding more bike lanes
organizing more community events like fairs and concerts

_____
_____

(5)
Playing in team sports is worthwhile because…
you learn to work with others
you get a lot of exercise
you learn new skills

_____
_____

2 Brainstorm main ideas for each topic. Circle the topic with the most main ideas. If both topics have the same number of ideas, circle both.

10 points each

(1)

A skill that should be taught at school
Wilderness survival
How to create a budget

_____
_____
_____

New column for the school newspaper
Advice column
Health column

_____
_____
_____

(2)

If I could be an animal, I would be…
an eagle
a dolphin

_____
_____
_____

I feel most proud when…
I do well on a test
I help my parents

_____
_____
_____

(3)

My personal goals for next year
Join a sports team
Practice my instrument more

_____
_____
_____

Challenges at school
Getting good grades
Getting along with everyone

_____
_____
_____

Hint: Choose a topic and main idea that inspires many ideas. If a topic is too narrow, you may run out of ideas to write about.

You have a lot of good ideas!

Five-Paragraph Essay
Topic Sentences

Level
★★
....

Score
/ 100

17

Date
/ /

Name

1 Choose four main ideas from page 32. Brainstorm the supporting paragraphs' main ideas.

5 points each

(1) **Essay's main idea:** I would like to live in New York City one day.

Main idea 1: Many museums

Main idea 2: Full of interesting and diverse people

Main idea 3: Beautiful buildings, bridges, and parks

(2) **Essay's main idea:** _____

Main idea 1: _____

Main idea 2: _____

Main idea 3: _____

(3) **Essay's main idea:** _____

Main idea 1: _____

Main idea 2: _____

Main idea 3: _____

(4) **Essay's main idea:** _____

Main idea 1: _____

Main idea 2: _____

Main idea 3: _____

2 Write a topic sentence for an introductory paragraph with the information from page 34.

20 points each

(1) **Topic sentence:**

> I would like to live in New York City one day because there are many museums, it is full of interesting and diverse people, and it has beautiful buildings, bridges, and parks.

(2) **Topic sentence:**

(3) **Topic sentence:**

(4) **Topic sentence:**

┌─ Don't forget! ─

An introductory paragraph's **topic sentence** is a sentence that describes the essay's topic and main idea, and the supporting paragraphs' main ideas.

This is a great start to an essay!

Five-Paragraph Essay
Topic Sentences

18

Level

Score

Date / /

Name

/100

1   Choose three main ideas from page 33. Brainstorm the supporting paragraphs' main ideas.

10 points each

(1)   **Essay's main idea:** New column for the school newspaper: advice column

     Main idea 1: Offers unbiased advice

     Main idea 2: Students can ask for advice anonymously.

     Main idea 3: Students can learn from one another's questions.

(2)   **Essay's main idea:** _____

     Main idea 1: _____

     Main idea 2: _____

     Main idea 3: _____

(3)   **Essay's main idea:** _____

     Main idea 1: _____

     Main idea 2: _____

     Main idea 3: _____

2 Write a topic sentence for an introductory paragraph with the information from page 36.

70 points for completion

(1) **Topic sentence:**

Our school newspaper should add an advice column because it can offer unbiased advice, students can ask for advice anonymously, and students can learn from one another's questions.

(2) **Topic sentence:**

(3) **Topic sentence:**

Don't forget!

An **introductory paragraph's topic sentence** should
- communicate the essay's topic and main idea
- express the supporting paragraphs' main ideas
- indicate the order of the supporting paragraphs

Can't wait to read more!

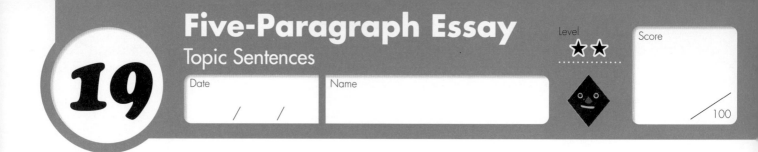

Five-Paragraph Essay
Topic Sentences

19

Level ★★

Score

/100

Date   /   /

Name

1 Write a topic sentence for each supporting paragraph with the information from page 36.

20 points each

(1) **Essay's main idea:** New column for the school newspaper: advice column

Topic sentence of supporting paragraph 1: The column can offer unbiased advice, which students often cannot get from friends or family.

Topic sentence of supporting paragraph 2: Sometimes people feel more comfortable asking for advice anonymously.

Topic sentence of supporting paragraph 3: Students often have similar problems, so they can learn from the advice column even if they don't ask for advice themselves.

(2) **Essay's main idea:** _____

Topic sentence of supporting paragraph 1: _____

Topic sentence of supporting paragraph 2: _____

Topic sentence of supporting paragraph 3: _____

(3) **Essay's main idea:** _____

Topic sentence of supporting paragraph 1: _____

Topic sentence of supporting paragraph 2: _____

Topic sentence of supporting paragraph 3: _____

┌─ Don't forget!

Each supporting paragraph in a five-paragraph essay will also include a topic sentence elaborating its main idea, which was introduced in the introductory paragraph.

2 Write a topic sentence for each concluding paragraph with the information from page 38.

40 points for completion

© Kumon Publishing Co., Ltd.

(1) **Conclusion's topic sentence:**

An advice column is an important addition to our school newspaper because it can offer neutral advice, students can write in anonymously to protect their identities, and we can all learn from the issues that are discussed.

(2) **Conclusion's topic sentence:**

(3) **Conclusion's topic sentence:**

Don't forget!

A concluding paragraph also has a topic sentence. It restates the essay's topic and main idea, summarizes the main ideas of the supporting paragraphs, and may draw a conclusion.

You are doing stellar work!

Five-Paragraph Essay
Outlining

Level ★★

Date
/ /

Name

Score
/100

1 Complete the outline format with words or phrases from the box. You can use each word or phrase more than once.

5 points each

Topic sentence of the conclusion	Concluding sentence
Summary of supporting paragraph 2	Topic sentence of the essay
Main idea of supporting paragraph 2	Conclusion
Topic sentence of supporting paragraph 3	Supporting detail

Introduction

Ⅰ. (1)_____

    A. Main idea of supporting paragraph 1

    B. (2)_____

    C. Main idea of supporting paragraph 3

Body

Ⅱ. Topic sentence of supporting paragraph 1

    A. (3)_____

    B. (4)_____

    C. Supporting detail

Ⅲ. Topic sentence of supporting paragraph 2

    A. Supporting detail

    B. Supporting detail

    C. Supporting detail

Ⅳ. (5)_____

    A. Supporting detail

    B. Supporting detail

    C. Supporting detail

(6)_____

    Ⅴ. (7)_____

    A. Summary of supporting paragraph 1

    B. (8)_____

    C. Summary of supporting paragraph 3

    D. (9)_____

Hint: An **outline** is a detailed plan for an essay. A five-paragraph essay outline should include the essential parts of the introduction, body, and conclusion.

2 Complete the outline with sentences or phrases from the box.

11 points each

> • When Baumgartner finally jumped, he broke the highest free fall record.
> • Baumgartner made history and contributed to science with this record-breaking jump.
> • Felix Baumgartner's space jump was a historic feat.
> • Flew in a capsule connected to a huge but delicate helium balloon
> • Reached a speed of 833.9 mph (1,342.8 km/h)

Introduction

I. (1)_____

    A. Broke the highest manned-balloon flight record

    B. Broke the highest free fall record

    C. First human to break the sound barrier in free fall

Body

II. Baumgartner broke the highest manned-balloon flight record during his space jump.

    A. (2)_____

    B. Rose 128,100 ft (39,045 m) above New Mexico

    C. Previous record for highest manned-balloon flight of 113,740 ft (34,668 m) was set in 1961

III. (3)_____

    A. His helium balloon had reached the stratosphere by the time he jumped.

    B. The stratosphere is the second layer of Earth's atmosphere.

    C. Joe Kittinger, Baumgartner's jump coach, set previous world record for highest free fall over fifty years ago

IV. Most notably, Baumgartner became the first human to break the sound barrier while in free fall.

    A. (4)_____

    B. Chuck Yeager first broke sound barrier in an experimental rocket airplane in 1947

    C. No one had broken the sound barrier while wearing only a space suit

Conclusion

V. After five years of training and preparing for his mission, Baumgartner made history with his landmark jump.

    A. Shattered the highest manned-balloon flight record

    B. Entered free fall from the greatest height ever recorded

    C. Broke the sound barrier during 4 minutes and 22 seconds of free fall

    D. (5)_____

_____

Just superb!

Five-Paragraph Essay
Outlining

21

Level
★ ★ ★

Date / /

Name

Score

/100

1 Brainstorm main ideas for each topic. Circle the topic with the most main ideas. If both topics have the same number of ideas, circle both.

10 points for completion

The biggest health risk for children is…

sports injuries

obesity

_____

_____

_____

_____ should be banned in public places

Smoking

Advertisements

_____

_____

_____

2 Choose one complete main idea from above. Brainstorm the supporting paragraphs' main ideas. Complete the outline for the introduction.

40 points for completion

Introduction

I. _____

    A. _____

       _____

    B. _____

       _____

    C. _____

       _____

Hint: You can use an outline to brainstorm ideas for your essay.

3 Write topic sentences for each supporting paragraph with the information from exercise 2 on page 42. Brainstorm supporting details for each main idea. Complete the outline for the body.

50 points for completion

Body

II. _____

    A. _____

        _____

    B. _____

        _____

    C. _____

        _____

III. _____

    A. _____

        _____

    B. _____

        _____

    C. _____

        _____

IV. _____

    A. _____

        _____

    B. _____

        _____

    C. _____

        _____

Those are great ideas!

Five-Paragraph Essay
Outlining

22

Level ★★★

Date / /

Name

Score

/ 100

1 Write the conclusion's topic sentence and concluding sentence with the information from exercises 2 and 3 on pages 42 and 43. Summarize each supporting paragraph's main idea. Complete the outline for the conclusion.

40 points for completion

Conclusion

V. _____

    A. _____

    B. _____

    C. _____

    D. _____

> **Don't forget!**
>
> A **concluding sentence** is the final statement of the essay's main idea. A concluding sentence may summarize or restate the main idea. It can also express a final judgment or opinion based on the arguments and evidence in the body of the essay.

2 Brainstorm main ideas for each topic. Circle the topic with the most main ideas. If both topics have the same number of ideas, circle both.

10 points for completion

The people with the most important jobs are...	If I could be anyone for a day, I would be...
teachers	the president
law enforcement officers	a pop star
_____	_____
_____	_____
_____	_____

3 Complete the outline based on one topic from exercise 2 on page 44.   50 points for completion

Introduction

I. _____

      A. _____

      B. _____

      C. _____

Body

II. _____

      A. _____

      B. _____

      C. _____

III. _____

      A. _____

      B. _____

      C. _____

IV. _____

      A. _____

      B. _____

      C. _____

Conclusion

V. _____

      A. _____

      B. _____

      C. _____

      D. _____

This is a great start to an essay!

23

Level ★★★

Score

Date   /   /

Name

/100

1 Read each supporting paragraph's topic sentence. Then put a check mark next to the detail that best supports the topic sentence. 10 points each

(1) A drama club would be a great addition to after-school activities.

_____ (a) A drama club gives students a chance to perform in front of others.

_____ (b) The bike team participates in races every year.

_____ (c) The drama club would not be popular with students.

(2) Global warming is a major environmental problem caused by human actions.

_____ (a) Energy-efficient buildings help conserve energy and use less fossil fuels.

_____ (b) Geothermal energy is the energy that is inside of Earth.

_____ (c) Earth is getting warmer because people are adding heat-trapping gases to the atmosphere.

(3) More modern novels should be assigned to students to read because they portray the world that students are living in.

_____ (a) Many classic novels include common themes that still have meaning today.

_____ (b) Some modern novels follow trends that may or may not pass the test of time.

_____ (c) Students can relate to the characters and circumstances of a modern novel more closely than with a classic novel.

> **Don't forget!**
>
> **Supporting details** explain, describe, or elaborate on a supporting paragraph's main idea. Supporting details can include facts, arguments, anecdotes, definitions, research results, and examples.

2 Read each topic sentence. Brainstorm three supporting details for each.   10 points each

(1) Vegetables are necessary for a healthy diet.

A. _____

_____

B. _____

_____

C. _____

_____

(2) Paper recycling should be mandatory at all schools.

A. _____

_____

B. _____

_____

C. _____

_____

3 Write supporting paragraphs using the topic sentences and supporting details from above.   25 points each

(1) _____

_____

_____

_____

_____

_____

_____

(2) _____

_____

_____

_____

_____

_____

_____

These are well argued!

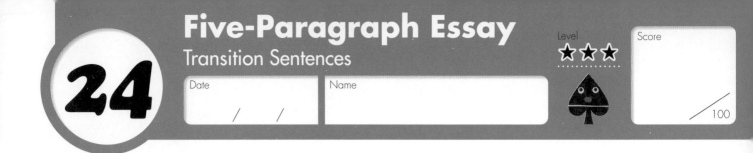

Five-Paragraph Essay
Transition Sentences

24

Level ★★★

Date / /

Name

Score /100

1 Read the two topic sentences. Then put a check mark next to the sentence that best transitions from the first topic sentence to the second.   10 points each

(1) Many students have a difficult time adjusting to middle school.

After-school activities offer a place to develop hobbies and meet others with the same interests.

_____ (a) Some students may join after-school clubs to make new friends.

_____ (b) Middle school teachers expect students to do more homework.

_____ (c) Football games are among of the most memorable events of the year.

(2) Many studies show that playing video games does not lead to getting bad grades.

Some schools have advised parents to limit the amount of time children play video games.

_____ (a) A person's judgment is influenced by his or her peers.

_____ (b) Video games have many pros and cons.

_____ (c) Despite the evidence of these studies, many adults still want to limit children's playing time.

(3) Citizens of certain countries must vote in elections or be fined.

When voting is mandatory, every citizen's voice is heard during the election.

_____ (a) Voter apathy is citizens' lack of interest in voting during elections.

_____ (b) While getting fined may seem extreme, it also encourages every citizen to be active in government.

_____ (c) Mandatory voting increases the cost of elections and can affect taxes.

Don't forget!

Transition sentences connect paragraphs and lead the reader from one idea to another. Transition sentences can convey what the two ideas have in common, how the two ideas differ, or how the second idea progresses from the first.

---

2 Read the two topic sentences. Then write a transition sentence that leads the reader from the first topic sentence to the second.

14 points each

(1) Building a new arena in our neighborhood would create terrible traffic.

Having an arena in our neighborhood would boost local business because more people would visit the area.

However, building a new arena would have benefits as well.

(2) Many experts disagree about what is the best meal to eat before running a marathon.

It may help runners to keep a food diary to document how different foods make them feel while running.

_____

_____

(3) Television and movies have linked winter holidays with the image of a snowy landscape.

Many people celebrate these holidays in places that are warm during the winter.

_____

_____

(4) Many teachers believe that using digital technology harms students' attention spans.

Researchers say no long-term studies have been done to prove this claim.

_____

_____

(5) Many birds fly into skyscraper windows just before dawn because the glass is hard to see and the buildings obstruct migratory flight paths.

Some groups conduct rescue and recovery missions and prod builders to consider bird safety when building new skyscrapers.

_____

_____

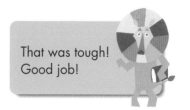

> **Don't forget!**
>
> Many transition sentences include the words or phrases *furthermore, likewise, consequently, moreover, hence, accordingly, nevertheless, conversely, on the contrary, incidentally, above all, next, meanwhile, with this in mind, generally speaking,* and *comparatively.*

That was tough! Good job!

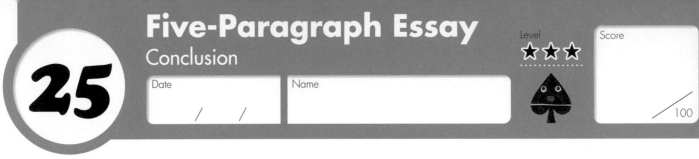

Five-Paragraph Essay
Conclusion

Date   /   /

Name

Level ★★★

Score   /100

1 Write a concluding paragraph with the information from each box. Restate the essay's topic and main idea, each supporting paragraph's main idea, and write a concluding sentence.

25 points each

(1)

> **Essay's main idea:**
>
> After a major disaster, several days may pass before essential public services can be restored, so people must be prepared.
>
> **Supporting paragraphs' main ideas:**
>
> • First, make a plan for surviving without help from others for at least seventy-two hours.
>
> • Next, make a kit of everything you might need, such as water, batteries, and nonperishable food.
>
> • Last, spread the word to your family and friends, and get involved with your community to ensure that others are prepared as well.

_____

_____

_____

_____

_____

_____

(2)

> **Essay's main idea:**
>
> If a female skier wants to race with the men's team, she should be allowed to do so.
>
> **Supporting paragraphs' main ideas:**
>
> • If her level of ability qualifies her for a race, her gender should not matter.
>
> • A race that included both genders would break down barriers between the men's team and the women's team.
>
> • The race would bring positive attention to both teams.

_____

_____

_____

_____

_____

_____

© Kumon Publishing Co., Ltd.

(3)

Essay's main idea:

Almost every country should have at least one public service broadcaster, or PSB.

Supporting paragraphs' main ideas:

- PSBs bring nations and people together with their programs.
- PSBs also pay particular attention to minority groups, which may be underrepresented in the media.
- PSBs offer accurate and impartial information that people can rely on.

_____

_____

_____

_____

_____

_____

_____

(4)

Essay's main idea:

Countries should use diplomacy to solve problems.

Supporting paragraphs' main ideas:

- Solving conflicts through discussions is less destructive than going to war.
- By discussing problems instead of going to war, countries encourage each other to negotiate.
- By continuing discussions, there is always a possibility that countries can come to a solution that benefits both sides.

_____

_____

_____

_____

_____

_____

Don't forget!

Many concluding paragraphs include the words or phrases _in conclusion, to conclude, finally, accordingly, consequently, as a result, therefore,_ and _in brief._

I conclude that you are quite clever!

Five-Paragraph Essay
Editing and Revising

26

Level ★★★

Score

/100

Date / /

Name

1 Read the draft of the introductory paragraph, which includes errors. Then complete each exercise.

40 points for completion

Multiculturalism should be embraced in a society. It increases our opportunities to learn from different people. Multculturalism also enriches our understanding of the world. Lastly people should not have to change their culture depending on where they life It seems that multiculturalism can be defined as when several cultures or ethnic groups live peacefully within a society. Toronto, Canada, is one of the most multicultural metropoltan areas, while also being one of the safest. When people are tolerant of each other's differences, they can learn a lot from one another.

(1) List the misspelled words with the correct spelling.

_____   _____

_____   _____

(2) Rewrite and correct the sentence with incorrect spelling and punctuation.

_____

_____

(3) Circle the most clear and concise sentence to replace the following excerpt from the paragraph: It seems that multiculturalism can be defined as when several cultures or ethnic groups live peacefuly within a society.

(a) Multiculturalism can be defined as several cultures or ethnic groups living peacefully within a society.

(b) Multiculturalism happens when cultures live within a society.

(c) A society is multicultural if different ethnic groups live there peacefully or when different cultures live together, too.

2 Complete each exercise based on the introductory paragraph on page 52.   20 points each

(1) Rewrite the "hook" sentence with the correct spelling.

_____

_____

(2) Write the transition sentence.

_____

_____

(3) Write a check mark next to each item that was present in the introduction.

_____ proper grammar

_____ correct spelling

_____ correct punctuation

_____ correct formatting, such as indentation

_____ clear and concise sentences

_____ a topic sentence

_____ three main ideas

_____ a hook

_____ a transition sentence

You can spot any error!

Five-Paragraph Essay
Editing and Revising

27

Level ★★★

Date   /   /

Name

Score

/100

1 Read the supporting paragraph, which includes errors. Then complete each exercise.

40 points for completion

By permiting multiculturalism, societies allow citizens to learn different cultural practices and ways of living from one another. When there is diversity, people can be introduced to different foods, religions, and lifestiles. For example, there is a large Amish community that lives in rural Pennsylvania in peace. The Amish are members of a religious group who live without many modern convenences, such as electricity and automobiles. Other residents of Pensylvania know a lot about him and their cultural practices. Many people admire their ability to live without modern comforts.

(1) List the misspelled words with the correct spelling.

_____   _____

_____   _____

(2) Rewrite and correct the sentence with incorrect grammar and spelling.

_____

_____

(3) Circle the most clear and concise sentence to replace the following excerpt from the paragraph: For example, there is a large Amish community that lives in rural Pennsylvania in peace.

(a) The large Amish community that lives in rural Pennsylvania is an example of a peaceful group.

(b) One example of multiculturalism, the Amish community is a large group that lives peacefully in rural Pennsylvania.

(c) For example, a large Amish community lives peacefully in rural Pennsylvania.

2 Complete each exercise based on the supporting paragraph on page 54.   20 points each

(1) Write one supporting detail with correct spelling and punctuation.

_____

_____

_____

(2) Based on the main ideas discussed in the introduction on page 52, write a transition sentence to the next main idea.

_____

_____

(3) Write a check mark next to each item that was present in the supporting paragraph.

_____   proper grammar

_____   correct spelling

_____   correct punctuation

_____   correct formatting, such as indentation

_____   clear and concise sentences

_____   a topic sentence

_____   supporting details

_____   a transition sentence

Don't forget!

Each supporting paragraph must have
- ✔ proper grammar
- ✔ correct spelling
- ✔ correct punctuation
- ✔ correct formatting
- ✔ clear and concise sentences
- ✔ a topic sentence
- ✔ supporting details
- ✔ a transition sentence

You have a good eye for this.

Five-Paragraph Essay
Editing and Revising

28

Level

Score

/ 100

Date / /

Name

1 Read the conclusion, which includes errors. Then complete each exercise.

40 points for completion

Societies that are multicultural have many benefits, and therefore multiculturalism should be embraced by the people in the society. Societies should encourage multiculturalism because it stimulates people to learn about different cultures, enhances our comrehension of the world, and allows people to continue their cultural practices and tradtions. When we learn more about one another we can has greater understanding of each persons perspective. Hopefuly this knowledge will create a more accepting and pieceful world.

(1) List the misspelled words with the correct spelling.

_____   _____

_____   _____

(2) Rewrite and correct the sentence with incorrect grammar and punctuation.

_____

_____

(3) Circle the most clear and concise sentence to replace the following excerpt from the paragraph: Societies that are multicultural have many benefits, and therefore multiculturalism should be embraced by the people in the society.

(a) A society that is multicultural is better off, and so multiculturalism should be allowed.

(b) Multiculturalism is very beneficial for a society and should be embraced.

(c) Societies that are multicultural have many benefits and therefore should be tolerated.

2   Complete each exercise based on the conclusion on page 56.

20 points each

(1)   Use words from the passage to complete the supporting paragraphs' main ideas:

(a) __Multiculturalism_____

_____

(b) __Multiculturalism_____

_____

(c) __Multiculturalism_____

_____

(2)   Rewrite the concluding sentence with the correct spelling and punctuation.

_____

_____

(3)   Write a check mark next to each item that was present in the conclusion.

_____   proper grammar

_____   correct spelling

_____   correct punctuation

_____   correct formatting, such as indentation

_____   clear and concise sentences

_____   a restated topic sentence

_____   three main ideas

_____   a concluding sentence

┌─ Don't forget! ──────────────────

Your conclusion must have
- ✔ proper grammar   ✔ clear and concise sentences
- ✔ correct spelling   ✔ a restated topic sentence
- ✔ correct punctuation   ✔ three main ideas
- ✔ correct formatting   ✔ a concluding sentence

Wow! You did it!

Five-Paragraph Essay

Date / /

Name

Score /100

---

1 Brainstorm main ideas for each topic. Circle the topic with the most main ideas. If both topics have the same number of ideas, circle both. 20 points for completion

Major League Baseball should...

let umpires use instant replay

lower ticket prices

_____

_____

_____

Schools should ban...

junk food from vending machines and cafeterias

cell phones

_____

_____

_____

2 Choose one complete main idea from above. Brainstorm the supporting paragraphs' main ideas. 30 points for completion

Introduction

I . _____

      A. _____

      B. _____

      C. _____

3 Write topic sentences for each supporting paragraph with the information from exercise 2 on page 58. Brainstorm supporting details for each main idea.

25 points for completion

Body

II. _____

    A. _____

    B. _____

    C. _____

III. _____

    A. _____

    B. _____

    C. _____

IV. _____

    A. _____

    B. _____

    C. _____

4 Write the conclusion's topic sentence and concluding sentence with the information from exercises 2 and 3 on pages 58 and 59. Summarize each supporting paragraph's main idea.

25 points for completion

Conclusion

V. _____

    A. _____

    B. _____

    C. _____

    D. _____

Great brainstorming!

Five-Paragraph Essay

30

Level
★★★

Date
/ /

Name

Score
/100

1 Complete the outline based on the information from brainstorming on pages 58 and 59. Develop your best ideas and refine your writing.

50 points for completion

Introduction

I. _____

    A. _____

    B. _____

    C. _____

Body

II. _____

    A. _____

    B. _____

    C. _____

III. _____

    A. _____

    B. _____

    C. _____

IV. _____

    A. _____

    B. _____

    C. _____

Conclusion

V. _____

    A. _____

    B. _____

    C. _____

    D. _____

This draft is so clever!

31

Five-Paragraph Essay

Level
★ ★ ★

Date   /   /

Name

Score

/100

1 Check your draft on page 61 for each item listed below. Correct any errors you may find.

50 points for completion

Your essay must have

_____   proper grammar

_____   correct spelling

_____   correct punctuation

_____   correct formatting

_____   clear and concise sentences

Your introduction must have

_____   a topic sentence

_____   three main ideas

_____   a hook

_____   a transition sentence

Each supporting paragraph must have

_____   a topic sentence

_____   supporting details

_____   a transition sentence

Your conclusion must have

_____   a restated topic sentence

_____   three main ideas

_____   a concluding sentence

2 Write the final draft of your essay with any necessary edits, cuts, and revisions.

50 points for completion

Fantastic essay!

63

Five-Paragraph Essay

32

Level ★★★

Score

Date / /

Name

/100

1 Brainstorm main ideas for each topic. Circle the topic with the most main ideas. If both topics have the same number of ideas, circle both.

20 points for completion

The Internet can...

threaten privacy

bring communities of like-minded people together

_____

_____

_____

Higher taxes should be paid by...

people who don't carpool

people who smoke

_____

_____

_____

2 Choose one complete main idea from above. Brainstorm the supporting paragraphs' main ideas.

30 points for completion

Introduction

I. _____

    A. _____

    B. _____

    C. _____

3 Write topic sentences for each supporting paragraph with the information from exercise 2 on page 64. Brainstorm supporting details for each main idea.

25 points for completion

Body

II. _____

    A. _____

    B. _____

    C. _____

III. _____

    A. _____

    B. _____

    C. _____

IV. _____

    A. _____

    B. _____

    C. _____

4 Write the conclusion's topic sentence and concluding sentence with the information from exercises 2 and 3 on pages 64 and 65. Summarize each supporting paragraph's main idea.

25 points for completion

Conclusion

V. _____

    A. _____

    B. _____

    C. _____

    D. _____

You are great at brainstorming!

33 Five-Paragraph Essay

1 Complete the outline based on the information from brainstorming on pages 64 and 65. Develop your best ideas and refine your writing.

50 points for completion

Introduction

    I. _____

        A. _____

        B. _____

        C. _____

Body

    II. _____

        A. _____

        B. _____

        C. _____

    III. _____

        A. _____

        B. _____

        C. _____

    IV. _____

        A. _____

        B. _____

        C. _____

Conclusion

    V. _____

        A. _____

        B. _____

        C. _____

        D. _____

2 Write the rough draft of your essay.

50 points for completion

You have a fantastic rough draft.

34

Five-Paragraph Essay

Date
/ /

Name

Level
★★★

Score
/100

1 Check your draft on page 67 for each item listed below. Correct any errors you may find.

50 points for completion

Your essay must have

_____ proper grammar

_____ correct spelling

_____ correct punctuation

_____ correct formatting

_____ clear and concise sentences

Your introduction must have

_____ a topic sentence

_____ three main ideas

_____ a hook

_____ a transition sentence

Each supporting paragraph must have

_____ a topic sentence

_____ supporting details

_____ a transition sentence

Your conclusion must have

_____ a restated topic sentence

_____ three main ideas

_____ a concluding sentence

2 Write the final draft of your essay with any necessary edits, cuts, and revisions.

_____

_____

_____

_____

_____

_____

_____

_____

_____

_____

_____

_____

_____

_____

_____

_____

_____

_____

_____

_____

_____

_____

_____

_____

Congratulations on a great essay.

1 Complete each sentence with the verb in the indicated tense.   10 points each

(1) **teach**

Our teacher _____ this topic before.   (present perfect)

Our teacher _____ math before switching to science.   (past perfect)

Our teacher _____ for ten years by the end of this year.   (future perfect)

(2) **send**

The writer _____ his scripts to Hollywood studios.   (present perfect)

The writer _____ scripts to his favorite directors already.   (past perfect)

The writer _____ his scripts before starting a new one.   (future perfect)

(3) **volunteer**

The boys _____ at the local park.   (present perfect)

The boys _____ at the park before school ended.   (past perfect)

The boys _____ at the park for one week by July.   (future perfect)

2 Complete each sentence with the verb in the present perfect, past perfect, or future perfect tense.   5 points each

(1) **paste**

My sister noticed that the address was incorrect, but we _____ the stamp on the envelope already.

(2) **set**

By the end of this race, the first runner _____ a new world record.

(3) **complete**

My brother offered to help with my science homework, but I _____ my assignment at school.

(4) **receive**

Jessie was happy all day because she _____ a letter from a faraway friend.

3 Write the type of dependent clause in each sentence: adjective, adverb, or noun clause.

5 points each

(1) My mom explained how to solve the math equation.   _____

(2) My dog, who has the sweetest brown eyes, begged for a treat.   _____

(3) The singer sang until her throat hurt.   _____

(4) The ball that bounced down the hall was a gift from my aunt.   _____

(5) Once the cat was gone, the mice came out of their hole.   _____

4 Complete each sentence in your own words with the indicated type of dependent clause.

5 points each

(1) _____, I listened to music.

[adverb clause]

(2) The banner _____ was heavy.

[adjective clause]

(3) We hope that _____.

[noun clause]

(4) She brushed her teeth _____.

[adverb clause]

(5) The teacher asked _____.

[noun clause]

You are almost at the finish line!

Review

Date / /

Name

Level
★ ★ ★

Score
/ 100

1 Complete the outline format with the phrases from the box. You can use each phrase more than once.

50 points for completion

Main idea of supporting paragraph 3	Topic sentence of supporting paragraph 1
Topic sentence of supporting paragraph 2	Topic sentence of the conclusion
Main idea of supporting paragraph 1	Summary of supporting paragraph 2
Summary of supporting paragraph 1	Main idea of supporting paragraph 2
Topic sentence of supporting paragraph 3	Summary of supporting paragraph 3
Topic sentence of the essay	Supporting detail Concluding sentence

Introduction

I. _____

   A. _____

   B. _____

   C. _____

Body

II. _____

   A. _____

   B. _____

   C. _____

III. _____

   A. _____

   B. _____

   C. _____

IV. _____

   A. _____

   B. _____

   C. _____

Conclusion

V. _____

   A. _____

   B. _____

   C. _____

   D. _____

2 Brainstorm main ideas for each topic. Circle the topic with the most main ideas. If both topics have the same number of ideas, circle both.

20 points for completion

One of my role models is...

my older brother

my neighbor

_____

_____

_____

If I could invent anything, I would invent...

a driverless car

an underwater city

_____

_____

_____

3 Choose a completed main idea from above. Brainstorm the supporting paragraphs' main ideas.

15 points for completion

Essay's main idea: _____

Main idea 1: _____

Main idea 2: _____

Main idea 3: _____

4 Write a topic sentence for an introductory paragraph with the topic and main ideas from above.

15 points for completion

Topic sentence:

_____

_____

_____

_____

_____

_____

Congratulations!
You finished!

1 Punctuation
pp 2,3

1 (1) :   (2) :   (3) :   (4) :

2 (1) : cumin, curry powder, and cardamom
(2) We learned a lot from Mr. Hall: loyalty, honesty, and teamwork.
(3) You can avoid the flu by taking simple precautions: washing your hands, avoiding sick people, and not touching your face.

3 (1) Daniel was happy: He knew that his dog would have a roof over its head.
(2) They needed six items to start: nails, wood, glue, roofing, sealant, and paint.
(3) The moment had arrived: The dog entered its new home and laid down.

4 [SAMPLE ANSWER] There were many ingredients in the recipe: tomatoes, onions, peppers, and cheese.

2 Punctuation
pp 4,5

1 (1) ;   (2) ;   (3) ;   (4) ;

2 (1) Sojourner Truth could neither read nor write; however, she could give speeches.
(2) The golfer practiced much more; hence, he won the championship.
(3) He was afraid of the dark; therefore, he shrieked when the power went out.

3 (1) He didn't have the stature that most athletes have; hence, he was told that he couldn't succeed in sports.
(2) Everyone had told him it was impossible; nevertheless, he persevered.
(3) When scouts arrived at a game, they ignored him; indeed, they thought he was too small for college baseball.

4 [SAMPLE ANSWER] He was small; however, he had determination and big dreams.

3 Vocabulary
pp 6,7

1 (1) smuggle   (2) smuggler

2 (1) talk   (2) play   (3) like   (4) shout

3 (1) embroider   (2) embroidery

4 (1) merchant   (2) merchandise
(3) extraterrestrial   (4) secrecy
(5) secretive   (6) terrain

5 (1) fearful   (2) angry
(3) secretive   (4) cheerful

4 Vocabulary
pp 8,9

1 (1) generate   (2) generator
(3) charge   (4) discharge
(5) calculated   (6) calculator

2 (1) calculator   (2) charge

3 (1) abstract   (2) concise
(3) expressive   (4) expression
(5) accomplishment   (6) accomplish

4 (1) celebrity   (2) magnet

5 Verbs: Present Perfect
pp 10,11

1 (1) move / moves   (2) have / has used
(3) have / has improved   (4) build / builds
(5) have / has reminded   (6) have / has made

2 (1) close / has closed
(2) finishes / has finished
(3) browses / has browsed
(4) operates / has operated

3 (1) Mom has started her job.
(2) Jonah has sliced bread for sandwiches.
(3) The realtor has sold many houses.
(4) I have finished my homework for tomorrow.
(5) I have turned off the lights.

4 (1) has not measured   (2) dislike
(3) has scorched   (4) has stumbled
(5) have sprouted

6 Verbs: Past Perfect

pp 12,13

1 (1) dislodged   (2) had fashioned
(3) had agreed   (4) ate
(5) had read   (6) had sprained

2 (1) had closed   (2) crossed
(3) celebrated   (4) saw

3 (1) The mirror had reflected the light.
(2) The game had stopped because of rain.
(3) The tree had concealed the big house.
(4) Maria had demonstrated the problem.
(5) Mom had thought I could make my lunch.

4 (1) filled   (2) didn't make
(3) had deleted   (4) had not confessed
(5) had delivered

7 Verbs: Future Perfect

pp 14,15

1 (1) will walk   (2) will have supported
(3) will have contained   (4) will sing
(5) will have finished   (6) will have won

2 (1) will have slept   (2) will clean
(3) will have collected   (4) will have read

3 (1) mom will have worked all week
(2) will have collected ten baseball cards
(3) I will have practiced for an hour
(4) will have demolished the building
(5) will have used all of the soap

4 (1) will have biked   (2) will have fluttered
(3) tutored   (4) will have reigned
(5) will have arrived

8 Review: Verbs

pp 16,17

1 (1) has walked / had walked / will have walked
(2) has promoted / had promoted / will have promoted
(3) have demonstrated / had demonstrated / will have demonstrated

2 (1) We have hiked through the sun-speckled forest.
(2) The boy will have camped all summer.
(3) Napoleon's army had forced a retreat.
(4) Lightning has struck a tree in the yard.

3 (1) had glanced   (2) will have raced
(3) had contained   (4) had generated

4 (1) had cleaned   (2) had deleted
(3) will have sewed

9 Review: Verbs

pp 18,19

1 (1) A   (2) C   (3) D   (4) B

2 (1) have not become   (2) had not collected

3 (1) Eli had not finished all his chores.
(2) Ignacio had not had an eventful winter.
(3) The company has not paid its taxes each year.
(4) The child had not listened to the story.

4 (1) has not broken   (2) had decided
(3) will have owned

10 Independent Clauses: Review

pp 20,21

1 (1) I went swimming   (2) we were never late
(3) The UFO landed
(4) we could not get a clear signal

2 (1) Because I missed the bus, I was late for school.
(2) When I finally got to school, the class was already working quietly.
(3) Everyone stared at me but didn't say a thing.
(4) The teacher did not give me detention because this was the first time I was late.
(5) If I arrive late again tomorrow, I will surely get detention.

3 (1) Sam will go to the party.
(2) The substitute teacher said that we could not leave.
(3) I would have returned the movie.
(4) We will go out for hamburgers.

4 (1) ✓   (3) ✓   (4) ✓

11 Dependent Clauses: Review

pp 22,23

1 (1) that the movie would become a hit
(2) why the sunset was so colorful
(3) how the motorcycle handles bad conditions
(4) how to do a back handspring
(5) That he was found guilty

2 (1) although it mentions real people
(2) until she found an illustration
(3) as though life were an adventure
(4) before cars could become widespread
(5) As she describes her home

3 (1) where I study art
(2) that the professor gave
(3) who received training
(4) who appears guilty
(5) that is held on the same track as the Daytona 500 auto race

4 (1) The building now has ramps
that students in wheelchairs use / adjective clause
(2) The article reports
that the man on trial was not guilty / noun clause
(3) Before writing was developed, people communicated
with smoke signals, drums, and whistles. / adverb
clause
(4) The pollution that results from car exhaust causes
major harm to our environment. / adjective clause
(5) My brother wondered
where all our friends had gone / noun clause

12 Independent and Dependent Clauses pp 24, 25

1 (1) where to go for our family vacation
(2) Before I could speak
(3) who always try to keep us from fighting
(4) I took my time reading and writing about my sister's choice
(5) She explained that my list had convinced her

2 (1) Most cats will not perform tricks, but Sunny can do many tricks.
(2) Sunny also plays fetch, and she loves to catch a ball.
(3) For example, she meows at strangers, so I keep her in my room when guests come by.
(4) She begs under the dinner table, but my mom won't let me feed her.
(5) My friends think Sunny is more like a dog than a cat, and I agree.

13 Independent and Dependent Clauses pp 26, 27

1 (1) Singing is my passion.
(2) I take care of my voice.
(3) I try not to talk or yell loudly.
(4) I avoid competing with her for solos.
(5) She is auditioning for the school's musical.

2 (1) adverb clause (2) adjective clause
(3) noun clause (4) adverb clause

3 (1) This is the closet where they keep all the costumes. / adjective clause
(2) James asked me why I make scrapbooks. / noun clause
(3) Before I joined the team, I watched too much television. / adverb clause
(4) The chemist showed us how rust forms. / noun clause

4 [SAMPLE ANSWERS]
(1) As we worked / As we walked
(2) that the boy wore / that the boy picked up
(3) before the picture was taken / before her father told her to
(4) who were from another school / who were on the math team
(5) what you know about a subject / what you have learned
(6) that I get all the answers correct / that I get a bike for my birthday

14 Five-Paragraph Essay: Review pp 28, 29

1 (1) B (2) A (3) C (4) C (5) C (6) D (7) E
(8) E (9) G (10) F (11) F (12) F (13) I (14) H

15 **Five-Paragraph Essay: Review** pp 30, 31

1 (1) Then, the engineer can use that information to improve the aircraft's design.
(2) engineers choose specific wind tunnels and adjust the powerful fans.
(3) Wind tunnels also move air at different speeds.
(4) what would happen if the aircraft were flying.
(5) When engineers build the model version of the aircraft, they include special instruments to take measurements during the wind tunnel test.
(6) They gather as much data as possible from these experiments for later examination.
(7) an engineer can predict how a full-size aircraft will perform.
(8) For example, an engineer might improve the flow of air around a vehicle to increase its lift and decrease resistance that slows it down.
(9) A wind tunnel is a powerful instrument for researchers.
(10) engineers have the ability to improve air travel and make great discoveries.

16 **Five-Paragraph Essay: Review** pp 32, 33

1 [SAMPLE ANSWERS]
(1) in San Francisco / in Tokyo
(2) make recycling mandatory / make carpooling mandatory
(3) species extinction / global warming
(4) cleaning up the park / fighting crime
(5) your teammates help you improve / you make friends and have fun

2 [ANSWERS MAY VARY: THE LIST(S) WITH THE MOST IDEAS SHOULD BE CIRCLED]

17 **Five-Paragraph Essay: Topic Sentences** pp 34, 35

1 (1) Essay's main idea:
I would like to live in New York City one day.
Main idea 1:
Many museums
Main idea 2:
Full of interesting and diverse people
Main idea 3:
Beautiful buildings, bridges, and parks
(2) [ANSWERS MAY VARY]
(3) [ANSWERS MAY VARY]
(4) [ANSWERS MAY VARY]

2 (1) I would like to live in New York City one day because there are many museums, it is full of interesting and diverse people, and it has beautiful buildings, bridges, and parks.
(2) [ANSWERS MAY VARY]
(3) [ANSWERS MAY VARY]
(4) [ANSWERS MAY VARY]

18 **Five-Paragraph Essay: Topic Sentences** pp 36, 37

1 (1) Essay's main idea:
New column for the school newspaper: advice column
Main idea 1:
Offers unbiased advice
Main idea 2:
Students can ask for advice anonymously.
Main idea 3:
Students can learn from one another's questions.
(2) [ANSWERS MAY VARY]
(3) [ANSWERS MAY VARY]

2 (1) Our school newspaper should add an advice column because it can offer unbiased advice, students can ask for advice anonymously, and students can learn from one another's questions.
(2) [ANSWERS MAY VARY]
(3) [ANSWERS MAY VARY]

19 **Five-Paragraph Essay: Topic Sentences** pp 38, 39

1 (1) Essay's main idea:
New column for the school newspaper: advice column
Topic sentence of supporting paragraph 1:
The column can offer unbiased advice, which students often cannot get from friends or family.
Topic sentence of supporting paragraph 2:
Sometimes people feel more comfortable asking for advice anonymously.
Topic sentence of supporting paragraph 3:
Students often have similar problems, so they can learn from the advice column even if they don't ask for advice themselves.
(2) [ANSWERS MAY VARY]
(3) [ANSWERS MAY VARY]

2 (1) An advice column is an important addition to our school newspaper because it can offer neutral advice, students can write in anonymously to protect their identities, and we can all learn from the issues that are discussed.
(2) [ANSWERS MAY VARY]
(3) [ANSWERS MAY VARY]

(20) Five-Paragraph Essay: Outlining   pp 40,41

1 (1) Topic sentence of the essay
(2) Main idea of supporting paragraph 2
(3) Supporting detail
(4) Supporting detail
(5) Topic sentence of supporting paragraph 3
(6) Conclusion
(7) Topic sentence of the conclusion
(8) Summary of supporting paragraph 2
(9) Concluding sentence

2 (1) Felix Baumgartner's space jump was a historic feat.
(2) Flew in a capsule connected to a huge but delicate helium balloon
(3) When Baumgartner finally jumped, he broke the highest free fall record.
(4) Reached a speed of 833.9 mph (1,342.8 km/h)
(5) Baumgartner made history and contributed to science with this record-breaking jump.

(21) Five-Paragraph Essay: Outlining   pp 42,43

1 [ANSWERS MAY VARY: THE LIST(S) WITH THE MOST IDEAS SHOULD BE CIRCLED]

2 [ANSWERS MAY VARY]

3 [ANSWERS MAY VARY]

(22) Five-Paragraph Essay: Outlining   pp 44,45

1 [ANSWERS MAY VARY]

2 [ANSWERS MAY VARY: THE LIST(S) WITH THE MOST IDEAS SHOULD BE CIRCLED]

3 [ANSWERS MAY VARY]

(23) Five-Paragraph Essay: Supporting Details   pp 46,47

1 (1) (a)   (2) (c)   (3) (c)

2 [ANSWERS MAY VARY]

3 [ANSWERS MAY VARY]

(24) Five-Paragraph Essay: Transition Sentences   pp 48,49

1 (1) (a)   (2) (c)   (3) (b)

2 (1) However, building a new arena would have benefits as well.
(2) [ANSWERS MAY VARY]
(3) [ANSWERS MAY VARY]
(4) [ANSWERS MAY VARY]
(5) [ANSWERS MAY VARY]

(25) Five-Paragraph Essay: Conclusion   pp 50,51

1 [ANSWERS MAY VARY]

(26) Five-Paragraph Essay: Editing and Revising   pp 52,53

1 (1) Multiculturalism, live, peacefully, metropolitan
(2) Lastly, people should not have to change their culture depending on where they live.
(3) (a)

2 (1) Toronto, Canada, is one of the most multicultural metropolitan areas, while also being one of the safest.
(2) When people are tolerant of each other's differences, they can learn a lot from one another.
(3) __✓__ proper grammar
_____ correct spelling
_____ correct punctuation
__✓__ correct formatting, such as indentation
_____ clear and concise sentences
__✓__ a topic sentence
__✓__ three main ideas
__✓__ a hook
__✓__ a transition sentence

(27) Five-Paragraph Essay: Editing and Revising pp 54,55

1 (1) permitting / lifestyles / conveniences / Pennsylvania
(2) Other residents of Pennsylvania know a lot about them and their cultural practices.
(3) (c)

2 (1) [ANSWERS MAY VARY] For example, there is a large Amish community that lives in rural Pennsylvania in peace. / Other residents of Pennsylvania know a lot about them and their cultural practices. / Many people admire their ability to live without modern comforts.
(2) [SAMPLE ANSWER] While multiculturalism helps us learn about our neighbors, it can also offer insights into the larger world.
(3) _____ proper grammar
_____ correct spelling
_✓_ correct punctuation
_✓_ correct formatting, such as indentation
_____ clear and concise sentences
_✓_ a topic sentence
_✓_ three main ideas
_____ a transition sentence

(28) Five-Paragraph Essay: Editing and Revising pp 56,57

1 (1) comprehension / traditions / Hopefully / peaceful
(2) When we learn more about one another, we can have greater understanding of each person's perspective.
(3) (b)

2 (1) (a) Multiculturalism stimulates people to learn about different cultures.
(b) Multiculturalism enhances our comprehension of the world.
(c) Multiculturalism allows people to continue their cultural practices and traditions.
(2) Hopefully, this knowledge will create a more accepting and peaceful world.
(3) _____ proper grammar
_____ correct spelling
_____ correct punctuation
_✓_ correct formatting, such as indentation
_____ clear and concise sentences
_✓_ a restated topic sentence
_✓_ three main ideas
_✓_ a concluding sentence

(29) Five-Paragraph Essay pp 58,59

1 [ANSWERS MAY VARY: THE LIST(S) WITH THE MOST IDEAS SHOULD BE CIRCLED]

2 [ANSWERS MAY VARY]

Hint: Choose a topic that inspires many ideas. If a topic is too narrow, you may run out of ideas to write about. A good topic choice will have three main ideas and some supporting details for each idea.

3 [ANSWERS MAY VARY]

Hint: Supporting details explain, describe, or elaborate on the supporting paragraph's main idea. Supporting details can include facts, arguments, anecdotes, definitions, research, and examples.

4 [ANSWERS MAY VARY]

Hint: Many concluding paragraphs include the following words or phrases: *in conclusion, in summary, in other words, as a result, consequently, for this reason, therefore,* and *thus.*

(30) Five-Paragraph Essay pp 60,61

1 [ANSWERS MAY VARY]

Hint: A five-paragraph essay outline should include the essential parts of the introduction, body, and conclusion. See page 40 for the parts of an outline.

2 [ANSWERS MAY VARY]

(31) Five-Paragraph Essay pp 62,63

1 [ANSWERS MAY VARY]

Hint: If you find editing difficult, try focusing on one feature at a time. For example, first check the whole essay for proper grammar. Then check the whole essay for correct spelling. Continue down the checklist until it is complete.

2 [ANSWERS MAY VARY]

(32) Five-Paragraph Essay
pp 64,65

(1) [ANSWERS MAY VARY: THE LIST(S) WITH THE MOST IDEAS SHOULD BE CIRCLED]

(2) [ANSWERS MAY VARY]

> Hint: Choose a topic that inspires many ideas. If a topic is too narrow, you may run out of ideas to write about. A good topic choice will have three main ideas and some supporting details for each idea.

(3) [ANSWERS MAY VARY]

> Hint: Supporting details explain, describe, or elaborate on the supporting paragraph's main idea. Supporting details can include facts, arguments, anecdotes, definitions, research, and examples.

(4) [ANSWERS MAY VARY]

> Hint: Many concluding paragraphs include the following words or phrases: *in conclusion, in summary, in other words, as a result, consequently, for this reason, therefore,* and *thus.*

(33) Five-Paragraph Essay
pp 66,67

(1) [ANSWERS MAY VARY]

> Hint: A five-paragraph essay outline should include the essential parts of the introduction, body, and conclusion. See page 40 for the parts of an outline.

(2) [ANSWERS MAY VARY]

(34) Five-Paragraph Essay
pp 68,69

(1) [ANSWERS MAY VARY]

> Hint: If you find editing difficult, try focusing on one feature at a time. For example, first check the whole essay for proper grammar. Then check the whole essay for correct spelling. Continue down the checklist until it is complete.

(2) [ANSWERS MAY VARY]

(35) Review
pp 70,71

(1)
(1) has taught / had taught / will have taught
(2) has sent / had sent / will have sent
(3) have volunteered / had volunteered / will have volunteered

(2)
(1) had pasted
(2) will have set
(3) had completed
(4) had received

(3)
(1) noun clause
(2) adjective clause
(3) adverb clause
(4) adjective clause
(5) adverb clause

(4) [SAMPLE ANSWERS]
(1) As I walked
(2) that the marching band carried
(3) we get ice cream after the game
(4) before she visited the dentist
(5) what we were talking about

(36) Review
pp 72,73

(1) Introduction
    I. Topic sentence of the essay
        A. Main idea of supporting paragraph 1
        B. Main idea of supporting paragraph 2
        C. Main idea of supporting paragraph 3
Body
    II. Topic sentence of supporting paragraph 1
        A. Supporting detail
        B. Supporting detail
        C. Supporting detail
    III. Topic sentence of supporting paragraph 2
        A. Supporting detail
        B. Supporting detail
        C. Supporting detail
    IV. Topic sentence of supporting paragraph 3
        A. Supporting detail
        B. Supporting detail
        C. Supporting detail
Conclusion
    V. Topic sentence of the conclusion
        A. Summary of supporting paragraph 1
        B. Summary of supporting paragraph 2
        C. Summary of supporting paragraph 3
        D. Concluding sentence

(2) [ANSWERS MAY VARY: THE LIST(S) WITH THE MOST IDEAS SHOULD BE CIRCLED]

(3) [ANSWERS MAY VARY]

(4) [ANSWERS MAY VARY]